SPORTS
A Pictorial Archive
of Contemporary
Illustrations

by Typony Inc.

DOVER PUBLICATIONS, INC. • New York

Copyright © 1982, 1989 by Typony Inc.
All rights reserved under Pan American and International Copyright Conventions.

Published in Canada by General Publishing Company, Ltd., 30 Lesmill Road, Don Mills, Toronto, Ontario.
Published in the United Kingdom by Constable and Company, Ltd., 10 Orange Street, London WC2H 7EG.

This Dover edition, first published in 1989, is an unabridged republication of the work originally published in 1982 by Van Nostrand Reinhold Company, New York, under the title *Sports Graphic Devices*. The illustrations on page 175 were not included in that edition.

DOVER *Pictorial Archive* SERIES

Manufactured in the United States of America
Dover Publications, Inc., 31 East 2nd Street, Mineola, N.Y. 11501

Library of Congress Cataloging-in-Publication Data

Sports graphic devices.
    Sports : a pictorial archive of contemporary illustrations / by Typony Inc.
        p.   cm.—(Dover pictorial archive series)
    Reprint. Originally published: Sports graphic devices. New York : Van Nostrand Reinhold, c1982.
    ISBN 0-486-26010-0
    1. Sports in art. 2. Drawing. I. Typony Inc. II. Title. III. Series.
NC825.S62S67 1989
745.4—dc19   89-31299
                                           CIP

Contents

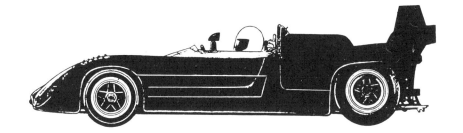

Basketball

Equestrian Sports

Fencing

Gymnastics

Ice Hockey

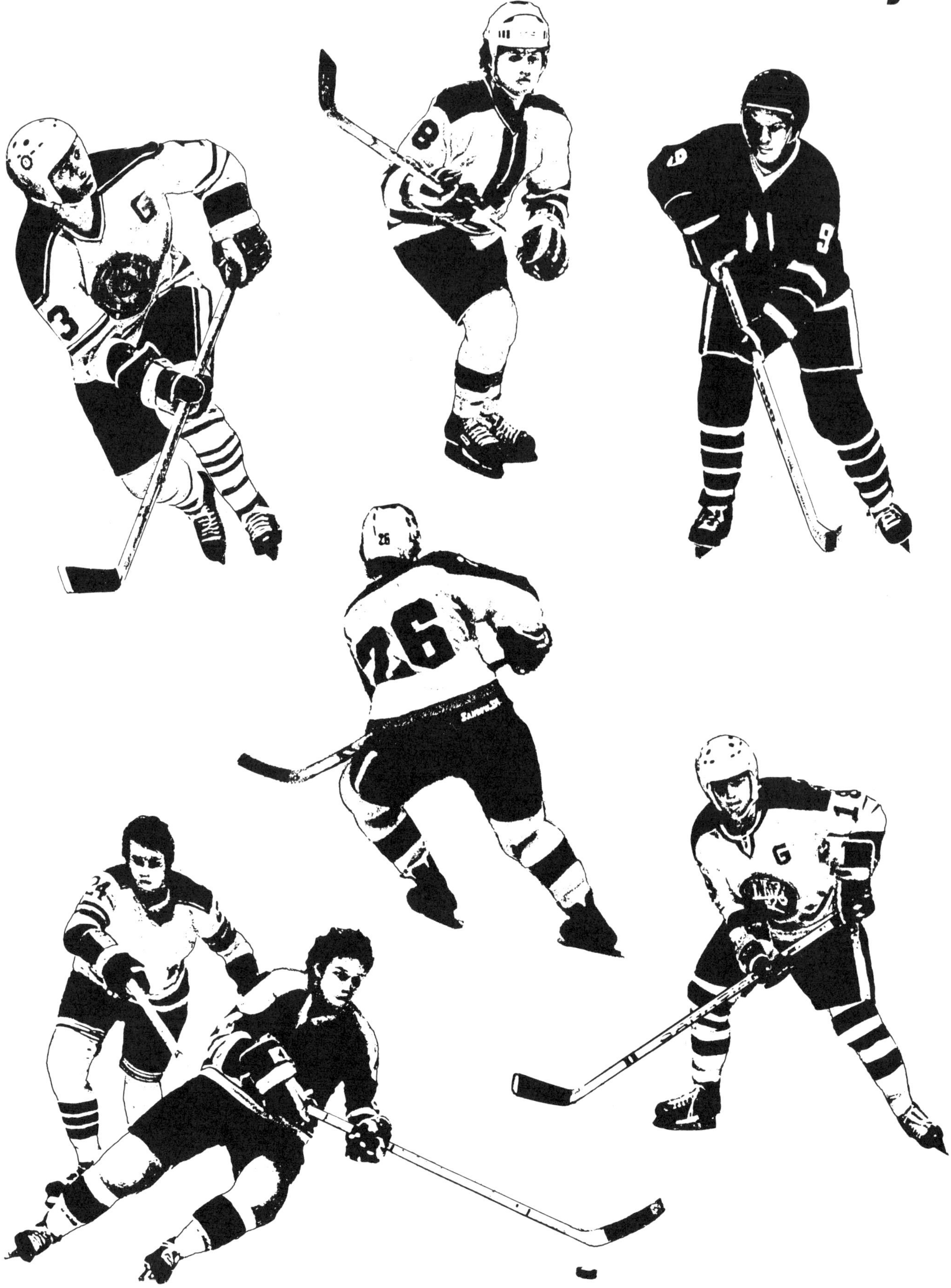

Polo

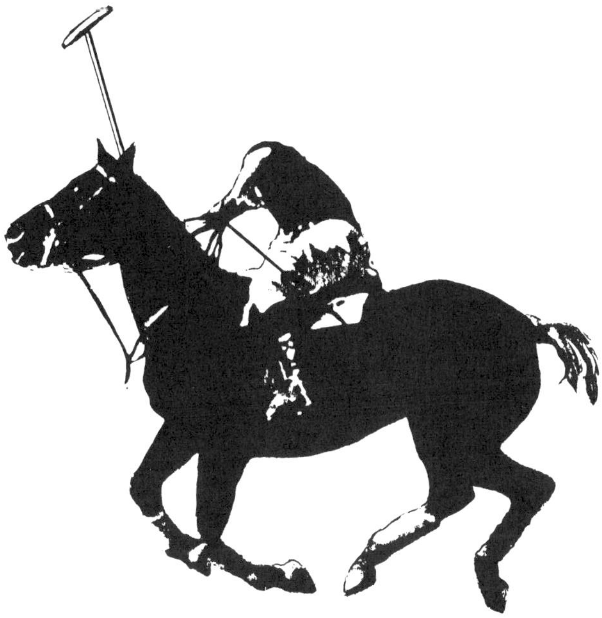

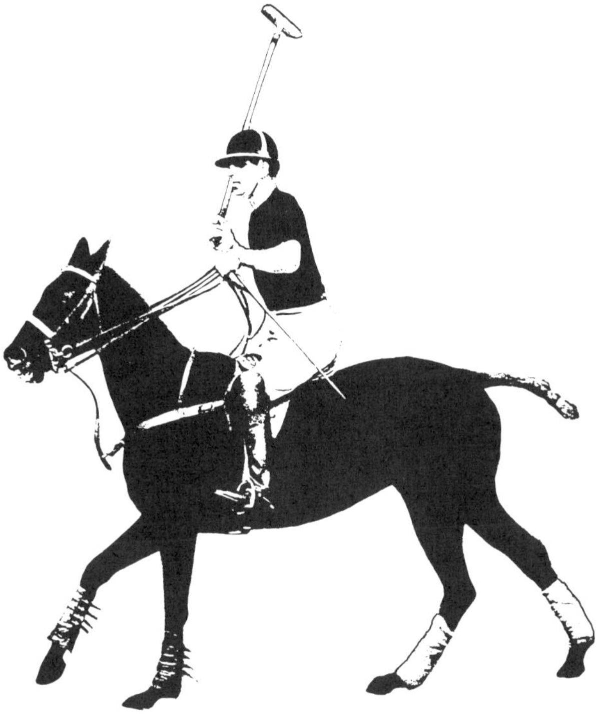

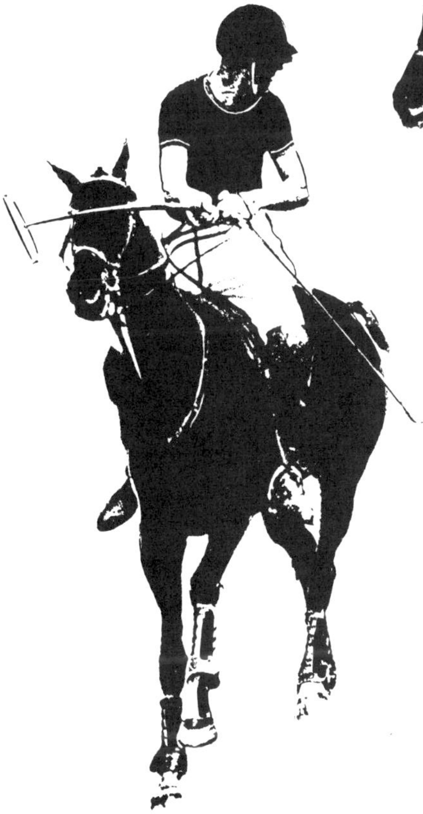

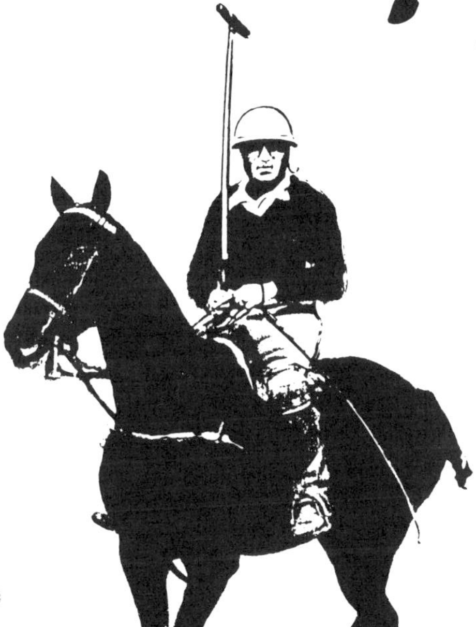

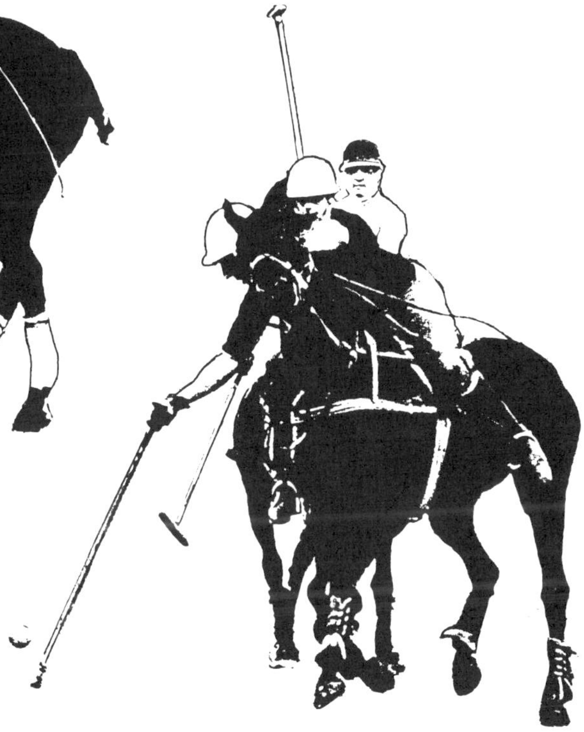

Skateboard

118

Skiing

Soccer

Swimming

Tennis

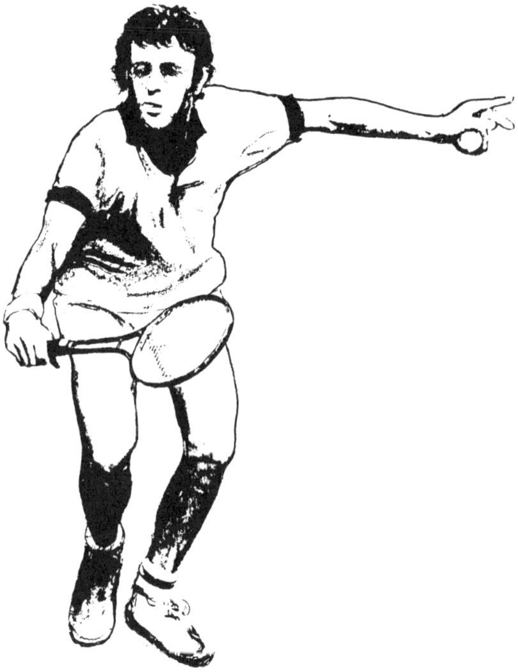

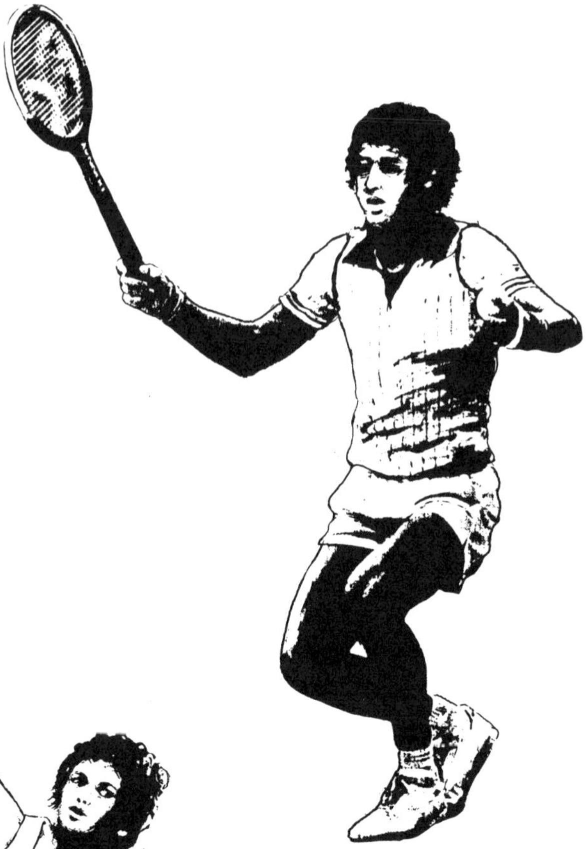

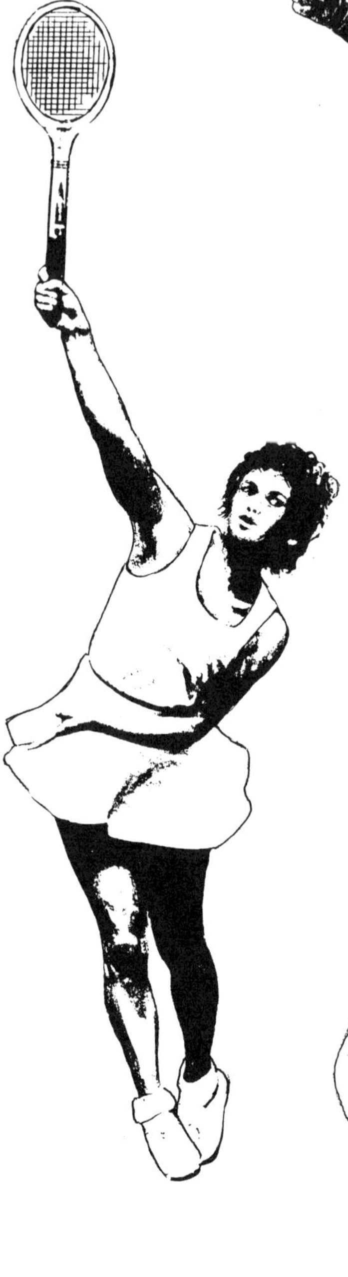

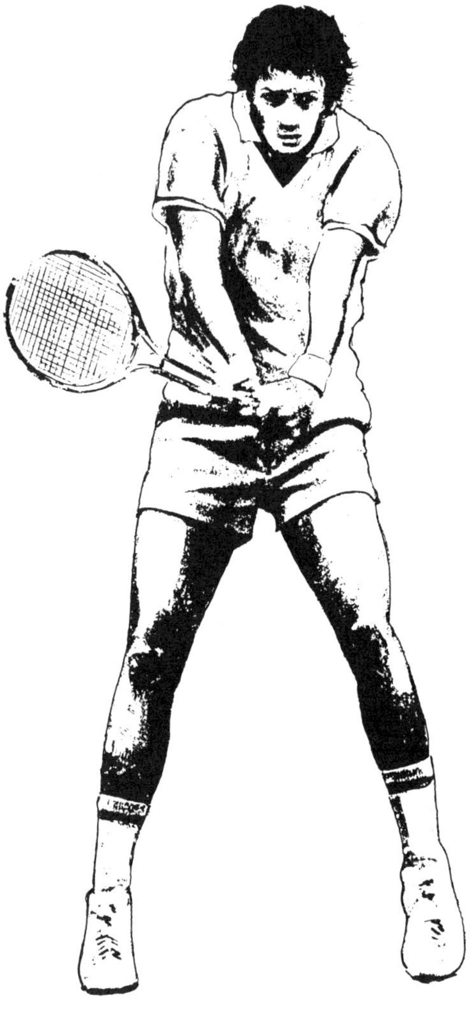

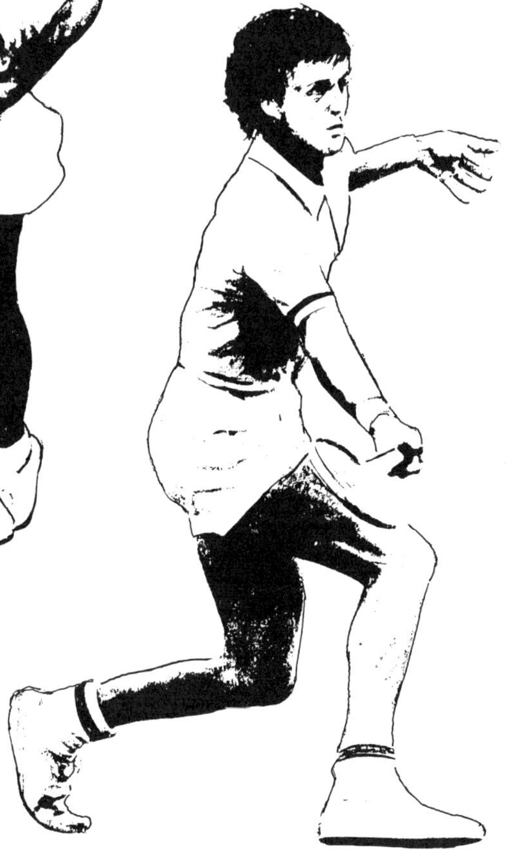

Weight Lifting

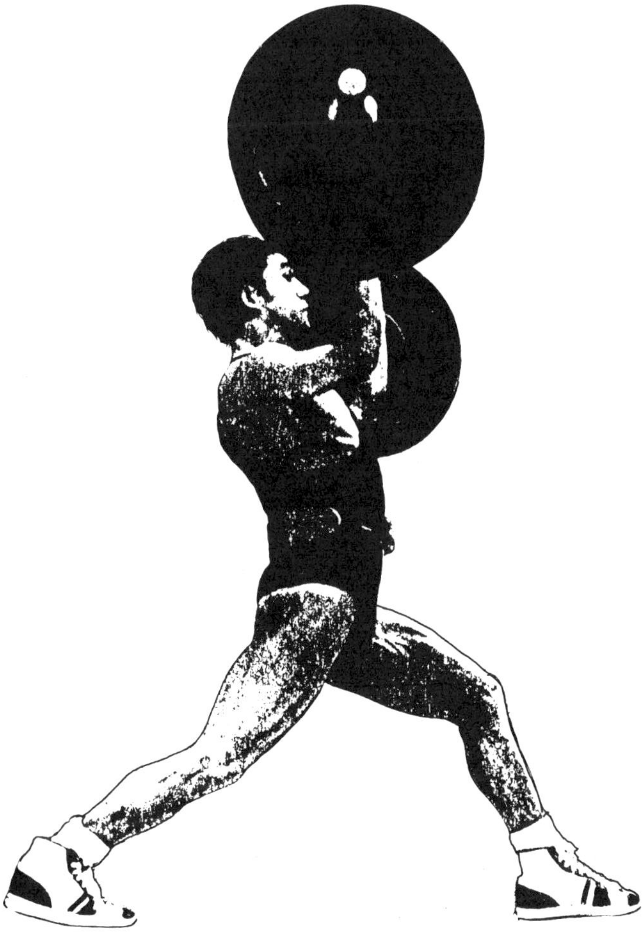

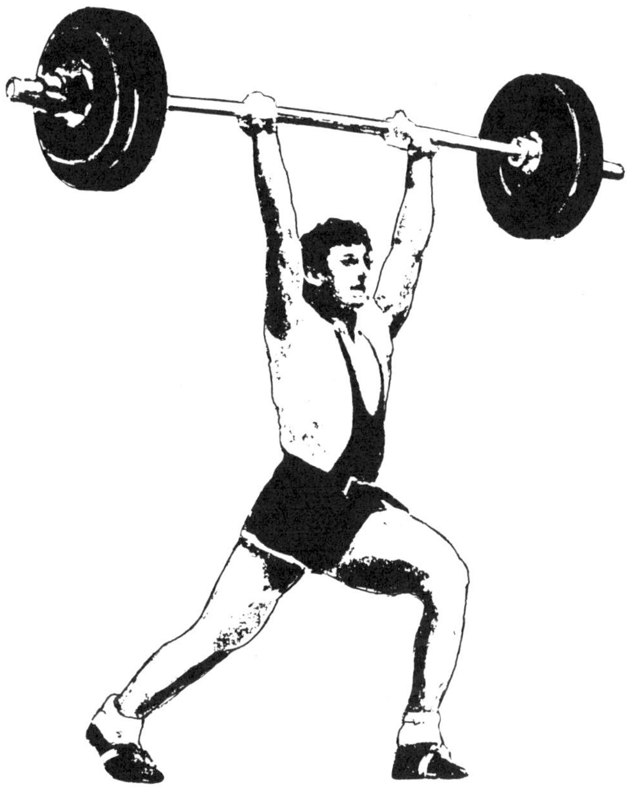

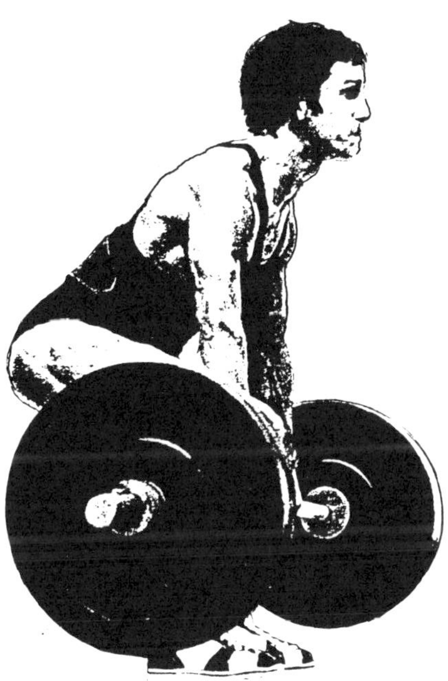

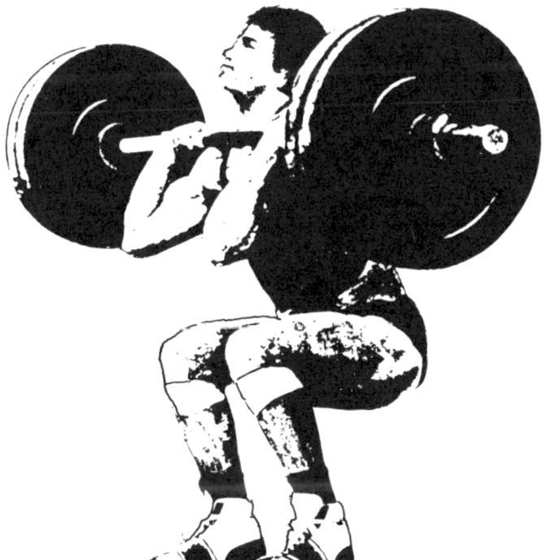

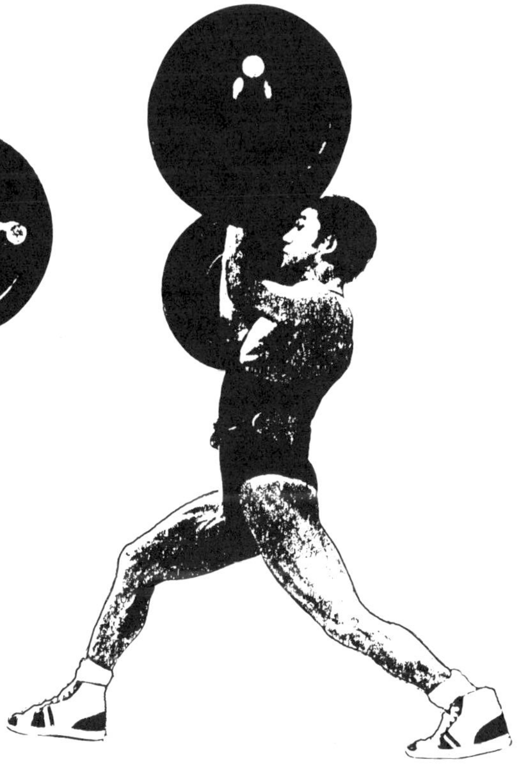

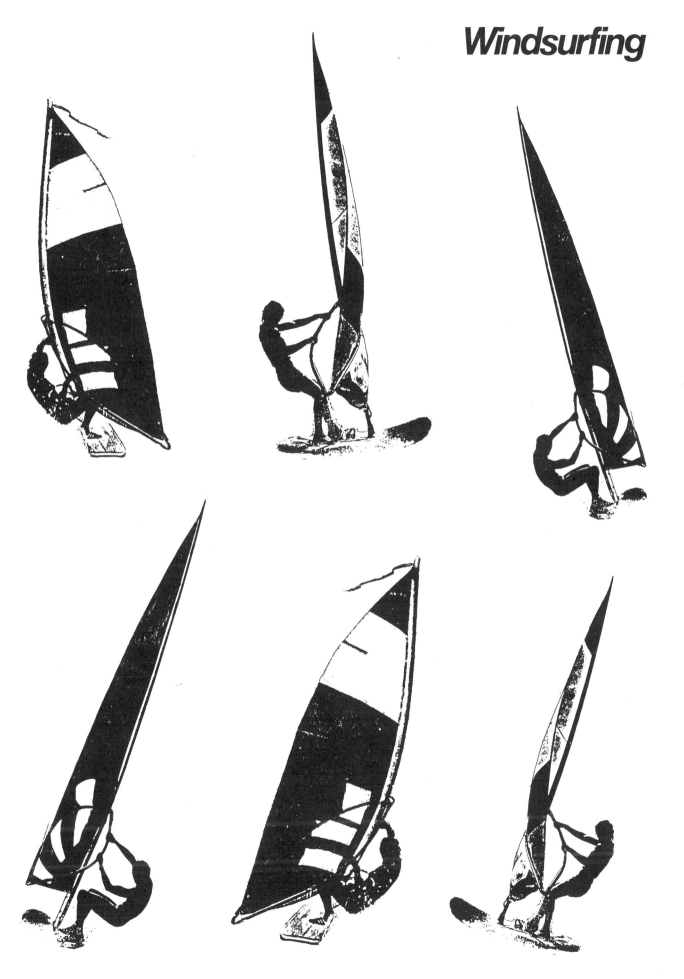